Holiday by the Sea

Heather Hammonds

Contents

Our Holiday Diary	2
The Tide Comes In	4
The Tide Goes Out	6
Under the Sand	8
A River	10
Wind and Waves	12
Rainy Weather	14
Glossary	16

Our Holiday Diary

My family had a holiday by the sea.
We stayed in a **holiday house**.

My brother and I made a holiday diary.
We took some photos and put them in our diary.

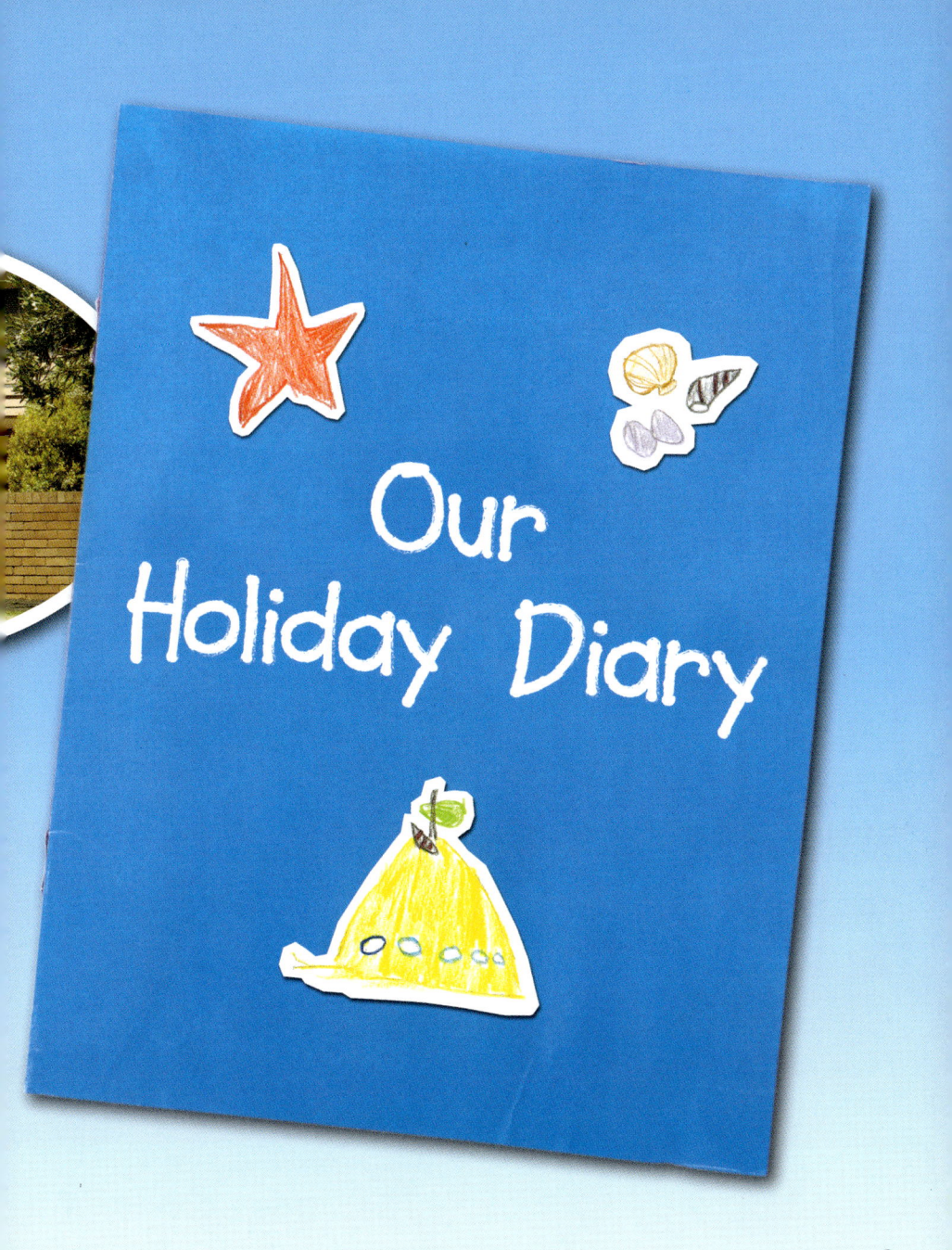

Our Holiday Diary

Day 1
The Tide Comes In

Today, we played in the sea. We saw that the waves were coming way up the beach.

The tide comes in

The waves splashed over the sand and the rocks. They splashed over our footprints in the sand.

Mum said the tide was coming in.

Day 2
The Tide Goes Out

Today, we had a picnic on the beach.
We saw that the waves were a long way out.
The sand and rocks were wet where the waves had been.

Mum said the tide was going out.
The tide goes in and out every day.

The tide goes out

Day 3
Under the Sand

Today, we went for a walk on the beach.
We saw some little holes in the sand, by the water.
Mum said **sandworms** had made the holes.
Sandworms live under the sand, on the beach.

Sandworms

# Day 4
A River

Today, we played
on the beach, by a river.
Water from the river went
on to the beach,
and into the sea.

A river

We saw some little fish
in the river.
The fish swam from the river
to the sea.

Day 5
Wind and Waves

It was very windy today.
The wind made lots of waves
on the sea.
Some of the waves
were very big.
We sat on the beach,
and looked at the waves.

We watched some **surfers** on the waves.

Surfers

Day 6
Rainy Weather

Today was the last day of our holiday.
It was a cold day.
The sky was grey.
The sea looked grey, too.

We saw some rain falling out in the sea.

It was time to go home.

A cold day

Glossary

holiday house

sandworms

surfers

16